Pickin' Stick

Building a Stringed Instrument

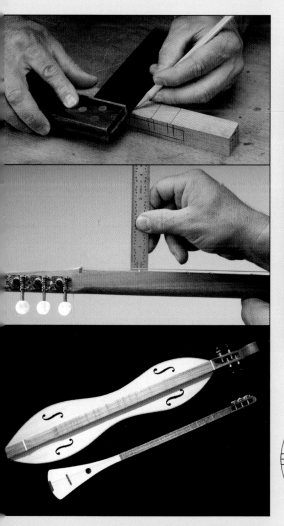

John Ressler

Schiffer Publishing Ltd®

4880 Lower Valley Road, Atglen, Pennsylvania 19310

Acknowledgments

Thanks to Corey Ressler for patiently working through many hours of photo sessions.
Thanks to Brent Peterson for making time for last minute photo shoots.
Thanks to Marc Adams who has opened many doors of opportunity for me.

Other Schiffer Books on Related Subjects:

The Fine Art of Marquetry, 978-0-7643-3499-3, $39.99

Making Wooden Boxes with Dale Power, 978-0-7643-0848-3, $14.95

Cover photo by Diane Scents

Designed by Mark David Bowyer
Type set in Myriad / Minion

ISBN: 978-0-7643-3571-6
Printed in China

Schiffer Books are available at special discounts for bulk purchases for sales promotions or premiums. Special editions, including personalized covers, corporate imprints, and excerpts can be created in large quantities for special needs. For more information contact the publisher:

Published by Schiffer Publishing Ltd.
4880 Lower Valley Road
Atglen, PA 19310
Phone: (610) 593-1777; Fax: (610) 593-2002
E-mail: Info@schifferbooks.com

For the largest selection of fine
reference books on this and related subjects,
please visit our web site at **www.schifferbooks.com**
We are always looking for people to write books on new and related subjects. If you have an idea for a book please contact us at the above address.

This book may be purchased from the publisher.
Include $5.00 for shipping.
Please try your bookstore first.
You may write for a free catalog.

In Europe, Schiffer books are distributed by
Bushwood Books
6 Marksbury Ave.
Kew Gardens
Surrey TW9 4JF England
Phone: 44 (0) 20 8392 8585; Fax: 44 (0) 20 8392 9876
E-mail: info@bushwoodbooks.co.uk
Website: www.bushwoodbooks.co.uk

Contents

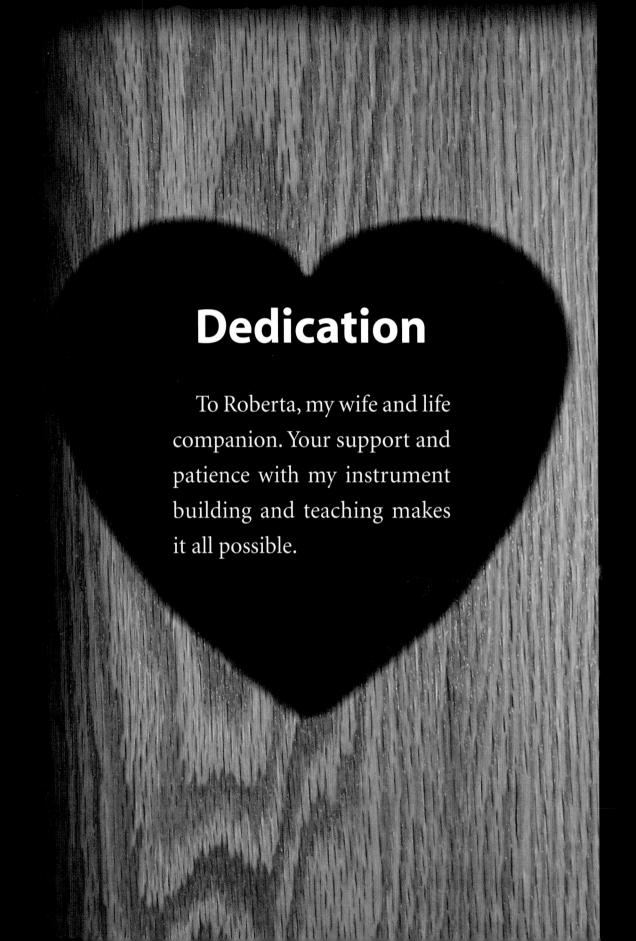

Dedication

To Roberta, my wife and life companion. Your support and patience with my instrument building and teaching makes it all possible.

Introduction
The Joy of Building Stringed Instruments

There are few things that give greater satisfaction than creating with your own hands. And few things bring greater joy than making music with an instrument that you have created yourself. Building stringed instruments combines precise joinery, creativity, and music all in one package. Hearing your creation make music for the first time will provide enthusiasm and satisfaction that will never grow old. For this reason, instrument building can become addictive!

While many people desire to build their own stringed instrument, the intimidation factor often prevents one from making the leap. At first glance, building a stringed instrument might appear to be out of reach due to the seeming complexity of the parts. The pickin' stick is an ideal instrument of choice to begin building stringed instruments.

This instrument is easy to build and can be completed as a weekend project. Although it is a fairly easy project, you will be exposed to the fundamentals of stringed instrument building such as building a sound box, fretting a fingerboard, installing an instrument nut and saddle, installing tuners, and stringing an instrument.

The pickin' stick is one of the simplest instruments to build and play, even for the non-musical craftsman. This is an ideal instrument for someone who has never played or built a stringed instrument before. You can easily learn the basics of strumming an instrument, playing notes, simple chord arrangements, and playing with others. Welcome to the world of stringed instrument building and get ready to create memories that will last a lifetime.

Chapter One
What is a Pickin' Stick?

A pickin' stick is a three-string fretted instrument with a solid neck and a hollow sound box, similar to a guitar. It is held and played in a similar position as a guitar is played, however, the fret placement and tuning are like those of a mountain dulcimer. Like a dulcimer, the pickin' stick is tuned to an open tuning, which means that it plays in one key, making it much simpler to learn to play. If you strum all of the strings on the pickin' stick, as long as it is in tune, it will sound right. Any note you play will sound good. While a guitar fingerboard consists of all half notes and allows you to play in all twelve keys, the frets on the dulcimer and the pickin' stick fingerboard are arranged in a diatonic scale, meaning that they are arranged as a combination of whole and half notes. This combination of notes means that any note that you play on the instrument will sound right since each note is a part of that key. In other words, you can play do-re-mi-fa-sol-la-ti-do up the fingerboard without skipping any frets as you would need to on a guitar.

The pickin' stick sound can be described as a cross between a mountain dulcimer and a banjo.

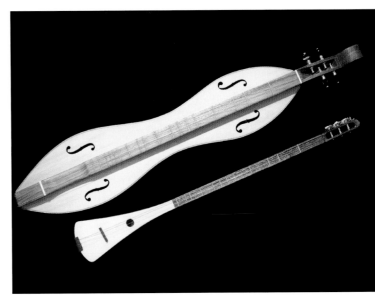

Comparing a pickin' stick to a dulcimer

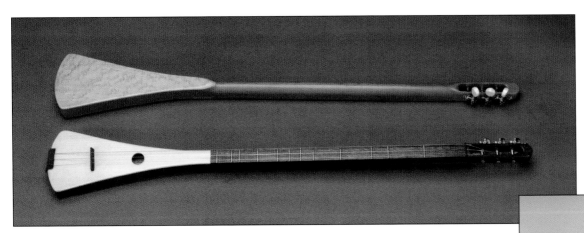

Pickin' sticks

Playing a pickin' stick

Before building or playing the Pickin' stick, it is important to know the parts that make up the instrument and their function.

Sound box: The sound box is a hollow chamber that provides a resonant cavity for the sound waves produced by the plucked string. It increases the volume of the sound.

Soundboard: The soundboard, sometimes referred to as the instrument top, vibrates as the strings are being plucked. The vibrations of the strings are transmitted to the soundboard through the saddle.

Sound hole: A round hole in the soundboard through which sound is projected.

Saddle: A piece of dense wood, bone, or plastic located on the sound box that defines one end of the instrument's scale length. It also transmits vibrations from the strings to the top.

Neck: The neck is the part of the instrument that goes between the sound box and the headstock. The pickin' stick neck, sound box sides, and headstock are one continuous piece. It is also part of the fingerboard.

Fingerboard: The fingerboard holds the frets into position and provides the playing surface on which the fingers depress the strings.

Strings: Steel strings are made of alloys including steel, nickel, or bronze. The strings are held under tension and when plucked provide the vibrations that drive the sound of the instrument.

Frets: Metal strips embedded in the fingerboard at specific points to change the length of the string, thus creating a specific note.

Nut: A piece of dense wood, bone, or plastic located between the headstock and the neck. The leading edge of the nut defines the other end of the instrument's scale length.

Headstock: The main function of the headstock is to hold the strings, which are attached to the tuners.

Tuners: Tuners are used to hold and apply tension to the strings.

End Pins: Brass brads are used to hold the strings at the end of the instrument.

Pickin' Stick Anatomy

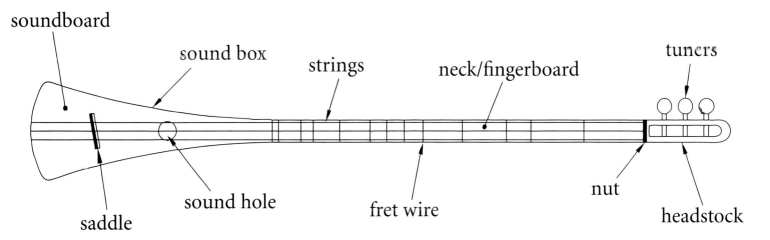

Chapter 2
Tools

Building a pickin' stick does not require a lot of specialty tools. The average woodworker will have most of the tools required to complete the instrument, such as chisels, files, rulers, squares, and clamps. There are a few specialty tools that will make the final set up procedures easier and we will discuss these in more detail as we get to those parts of the instrument. If you need to purchase some tools it makes sense to purchase the best quality tools you can afford. The old adage that you get what you pay for is true. Better to have a few high quality tools than many poorly made ones. As you develop your instrument building skills you can begin to add to your collection.

The tools shown here are what you will use the most for building your pickin' stick. Although the instrument could be made entirely with hand tools, a number of power tools will make some of the tasks much easier.

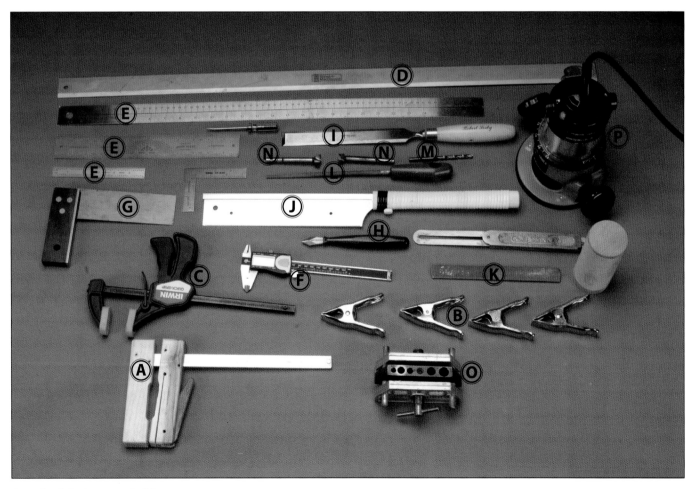

General tools for instrument building

Clamps

You will need to have about twelve clamps on hand. The clamping procedures in building stringed instruments require only light pressure, so you should avoid hand screw type clamps, which can dent the wood or break the instrument. Wooden cam type clamps (A) are ideal for instrument building. They produce pressure as the cam lever is rotated, causing the jaw to close, and provide just the right amount of force to secure well fitted parts. Several small spring clamps (B) work best for clamping some of the smaller parts. You will find that Quick Grip® type clamps (C) are useful as well.

Layout and Measuring Tools

A variety of layout tools will be necessary for accurately measuring and marking the critical points of the instruments. A straight edge (D) that is at least two feet long is useful in determining how straight the neck is and drawing center lines on the instrument. Rulers of various lengths (E) are needed to lay out the frets, measure string height and length, and locate the critical points along the length of the instrument. A digital caliper (F) is required to accurately measure fret locations and is used to measure the thickness of the parts. The square (G) is used to lay out 90 degree lines and to check that surfaces are 90 degrees to each other. A marking knife (H) or scratch awl is preferred over a pencil for marking critical fret locations and layout lines or hole locations.

Cutting Tools

A straight chisel is used for finishing cuts that cannot be cut clean with a power tool. A one-inch-wide paring chisel (I) is the chisel of choice for instrument building. The Japanese style pull saw (J) is used for cutting fret slots and trimming parts to length. A saw with a blade that cuts a .023" kerf will work best for this project, as it can be used to cut the fret slots as well as cut parts. The 4-in-1 half round file (K) is a good choice for shaping the back where it blends with the body. Finally, a 1/4" to 3/8" course, round file (L) works well for shaping the headstock.

Drilling

Although all of the drilling can be accomplished with a hand drill, a drill press will make the drilling tasks much easier and more accurate. You will need a 1/4" and 3/8" twist bit (M) or brad point bit for drilling for the tuner posts and the headstock slot. A 5/8" and 3/4" flat bottom bit (N) is used for drilling holes for the sound box and the sound hole. A doweling jig (O) helps to drill holes on center and keeps the bit straight when drilling out the headstock.

Power Tools

Power tools are not necessary, but they make the process much easier and produce more accurate results. A table saw would be the most difficult power tool to do without. This will be used to rip the stock for the neck. A router (P) is used for flush trimming the top and back to the sides, cleaning out the headstock slot, and rounding over the backside of the neck. A flush trim router bit and a 1/2" round over router bit will be used for these processes. A drill press will create accurate, straight holes. And a disc sander can be used to help shape parts. A band saw is used for cutting radius parts, such as the end block, and provides a safer alternative for the ripping operations. If you don't own these power tools, a good resource is your local woodworking clubs. Many of these groups make tools available to their members.

The key to getting the most out of your tools is to keep them sharp. There are many methods of sharpening described in books dedicated to this subject, or you can view techniques online. Sharp tools are the safest tools and produce the highest quality results.

Chapter 3
Material Selection

The materials for the pickin' stick are simple and easily obtained. All materials should be well seasoned and kiln dried. Since wood is made up of a series of open cells, it is always collecting and dissipating moisture to come into equilibrium with the atmosphere, even after proper drying and storage. This causes the wood to expand and contract which can distort the instrument, making it difficult or impossible to set up or play properly. Be particular in your wood selection and storage, and you will be rewarded with a trouble-free instrument.

Pickin' stick materials

Selecting Material for the Neck

The first step in selecting material for the neck is to decide what wood species to use. It is best to select a closed grain wood species such as walnut, maple, or cherry. Closed grain means that the wood cells are small, which makes the wood denser and smoother to the touch. Since the neck of the pickin' stick is also the fingerboard, we want the wood to be as smooth as possible, so your fingers will glide easily from one fret to another. Because of this, oak or ash would not be a good choice. For our project we will be using walnut. This wood species is easy to cut, shape, and sand. It also finishes beautifully with little effort.

Quartersawn board

Plainsawn board

Grain Orientation

It is best to select stock for the neck that is quartersawn. This grain configuration will minimize wood movement, making it less likely to warp. Quartersawn means that its grain runs at right angles to the surface of the board. A plainsawn board has grain that runs parallel with the surface of the board. The examples shown here are oak, which shows the grain structure the best.

Since our neck is 7/8" wide, we will need a quartersawn board that is 1 1/16" thick, from which we will rip a 7/8" wide strip for the neck. If you have a plainsawn board, you can achieve the same thing by using a board that is 7/8" thick to rip a 1 1/16" wide strip.

It is critical at this point to check the straightness of the neck. Use a long straightedge to check all surfaces. You will also want to check to make sure the neck isn't twisted. To check this, lay it on a flat table or workbench. Try to rock it from side to side. If it wobbles, the neck is twisted.

Checking the straightness of the neck

If the neck is only slightly bowed or twisted, it can be straightened by placing a strip of self-adhesive sandpaper to a flat surface and sanding the neck until it is perfectly flat.

Flattening a slightly bowed neck

If it is more than slightly bowed or twisted, it is best to set it aside and find a new board. The neck is the foundation of the instrument and it will be difficult to proceed if it is not straight and flat.

Selecting Material for the Back and Top

The material for the back can match the wood used for the neck, or it can be a different wood species. I like to use contrasting wood with a lot of figure in the grain, such as the flamed maple back shown here, which gives a striking visual effect. This is a good place to use your creativity when building your instrument.

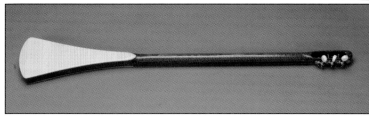

Flamed maple back

Although the top could be made from hardwood, quartersawn spruce is the wood of choice for instrument tops. Sitka spruce has a high strength to weight ratio, making it the toughest member of the spruce family. The strength of spruce allows the top to be sanded down very thin, which allows maximum vibration. Cedar and fir are also excellent choices for top material. Tops can be purchased as guitar tops or dulcimer tops from luthier suppliers or from material at the lumberyard. If you purchase from a lumberyard, be very particular about what piece you select. Make sure it is quartersawn for maximum strength and that it is good and dry before attempting to use it as an instrument top.

Quartersawn Sitka spruce

Quartersawn cedar

Selecting Material for the Nut and Saddle

The nut and saddle should be made of very dense hardwood. Since the strings ride over the top of these parts and slide back and forth in the slots when the instrument is tuned, they can wear out quickly if a softer wood is used. When the strings are plucked, the vibrations are transmitted to the top and to the neck. A dense nut and saddle are necessary to keep the tone of the instrument bright. Softer wood can absorb the vibrations, causing the sound to be muted. I like to use Ipe for the nut and saddle. Ipe is a very dense hardwood. It also is somewhat oily, which provides a natural lubricant for the strings. If you do not have access to this wood species, you can use maple or some other similar hardwood. Bone can also be used in place of wood for the nut.

Material List

Here is a complete list of parts needed for your project. Take the time to gather and prepare all of the materials to these dimensions before you start the building process. If you need to stop in the middle of the assembly process to run to the hardware store or find a board for a part, you will quickly lose your momentum and concentration as you are building your instrument.

Qty	Part	Thickness	Width	Length	Material
1	Neck	1 1/16"	7/8"	31"	Walnut
1	End block	15/16"	1 1/4"	4 5/16"	Walnut
1	Back	1/8"	4 1/4"	12"	Maple
1	Top	1/8"	4 1/4"	12"	Sitka spruce
1	Nut	1/8"	1/4"	1 1/4"	Dense hardwood or bone
1	Saddle	3/16"	1/4"	1 3/8"	Dense hardwood
12"	Medium fretwire				
3	Brass brads				
1	Brass eye screw				
1 Set	Mandolin tuners				
1 Set	Mandolin strings				
3	#2 x 1/4" screws				

In addition to these parts, you will need a bottle of thin cyanoacrylate glue (super glue) and a bottle of aliphatic resin glue such as Titebond®.

Chapter 4
Before You Begin

I know you are anxious to begin building, but before you start making sawdust, take some time to plan your work and make preparations for your project. Read this book from start to finish and make sure you have a general understanding of each of the steps. Be able to visualize the final product so you have a clear picture in your mind of what you are making. Make some notes as you review the processes to serve as a reminder of the tools or parts that you might need to procure before starting. It is helpful if you make a list of all of the steps in the order that they need to be completed. You can use this as a checklist as you work through this project.

Gather your tools together and test them on some scrap wood to make sure they are sharp and in good condition. If your tools are dull, take the time to sharpen your tools before you begin the project. Once you get started, your enthusiasm for building the instrument will tempt you to neglect sharpening your tools. Dull tools are difficult to work with and pose a greater danger than sharp tools.

Instrument Building Practices

There are several principles to keep in mind as you build your instrument and if followed, they will help to ensure your success.

Shop Safety

The best advice I can give you before you begin building instruments is to work safely. Once your instrument is complete, you will want all of your fingers to play your pickin' stick, so work in a manner that will ensure that you will keep all of your digits. Keep in mind that safety is a way of working, not just a list of rules to follow. The following reminders will help ensure an enjoyable building and playing experience:

- Wear safety glasses and make sure the lenses are clean.
- Always keep your fingers between three and six inches away from saw blades while they are running.
- Do not work when you are tired or stressed.
- Work in a well lit area.
- Keep your work area clean.
- Do not wear loose clothing while operating woodworking machinery.
- Never leave a machine running unattended.
- Be aware of where your hands are at all times. Keep them away from blades at all times.
- When using a chisel, keep your hands behind the cutting edge at all times.
- If the little voice in your head is telling you that you probably should not be doing something, don't do it.

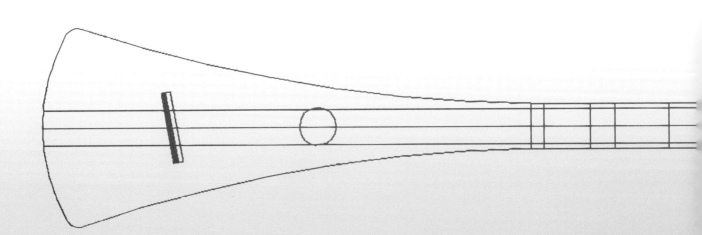

Center Line

When laying out the parts of the pickin' stick, you should always work off of the parts' center line. This will keep the instrument symmetrical and give it a professional appearance. Keep this in mind, especially when gluing on the top, installing the end pins, and cutting out the headstock. If you do not pay attention to making sure the parts line up on the center of the instrument, it is likely that the strings will not follow the fingerboard.

Humidity

When building wood instruments, it is important to maintain a level of humidity and temperature that will keep the wood parts stabilized. Too much relative humidity in the workshop can make parts swell. If the air is too dry, the wood can shrink and crack. An ideal environment for your workshop is around 40-50 percent relative humidity with an average temperature of about 70 degrees. You can measure relative humidity with a hygrometer. Make adjustments as needed using a humidifier or dehumidifier. An instrument built under less than ideal conditions can experience structural damage and string adjustment issues.

Work Habits

The way you approach instrument building can contribute to the success or failure of the project. Keep in mind that every step in the building process is critical. Think through the process before you start cutting. Understand why you are doing a particular task and what the final result is supposed to be. Be particular in how you work. Take your time to cut parts carefully and accurately. Keep your hands clean and avoid smearing glue on areas of the instrument that are exposed. Most importantly, enjoy the instrument building process. Following good work habits will not only ensure the success of the finished product, but will also give you a sense of pride and satisfaction.

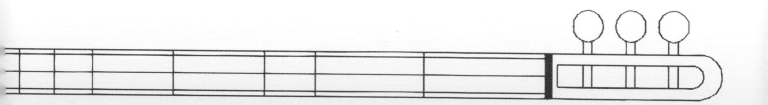

Chapter 5
Laying Out the Lines

The first step of this project is to accurately lay out all of the cut lines and fret locations on the neck. Set aside enough time to complete the entire layout at one time. It is easy to make mistakes when you stop part way through. Start at the headstock and work your way to the end of the instrument. The extra length at the end of the neck will be trimmed off after the end block is glued into place.

Top View

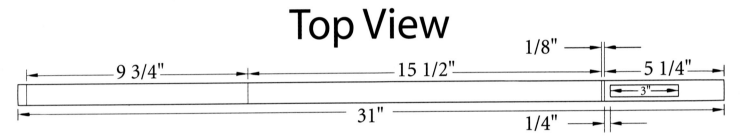

Using the neck that you have already cut to size, measure down 5 1/4" from the headstock end. This will be the location of the backside of the nut. Make a square line across the width of the neck. Measure down another 1/8" and draw another line. Fill in between these two lines with pencil to mark the location of the nut.

Measuring nut location

Marking line across neck

From the backside of the nut, measure up 1/4" to mark the location of the bottom end of the tuner slot in the headstock. From this point, measure up another 3" to mark the top end. From the center line, mark the width of the slot 1/2" wide. Connect all of the lines to form a rectangle. At this point the end of the headstock is longer than the final dimension. We will trim this during the final headstock shaping process.

Marking the nut location

Marking the headstock slot

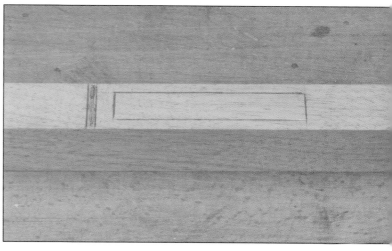

Final layout of headstock slot

17

Now measure the location where the soundboard meets the fingerboard. For this dimension, hold your ruler at the front side of the nut. Measure down 15 1/2" and make a mark. Square a line across the neck. From this point, measure down another 9 3/4". This will mark the location of the end block. For the end block mark, you will need to extend this mark down the sides of the instrument. Since we will be cutting this area out for the top, we will need to preserve the line by extending this mark down the sides of the instrument. If you are building more than one instrument, you might find a story stick will save some time. A story stick has all of the dimensions of the instrument laid out so you can clamp it in place on the neck and create all of your layout lines from it.

Marking the end block location

Measuring from face side of nut

Completed Initial Layout

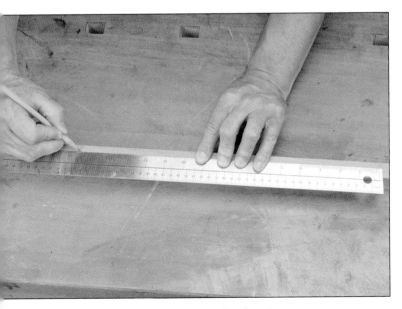

Marking the location where top meets fingerboard

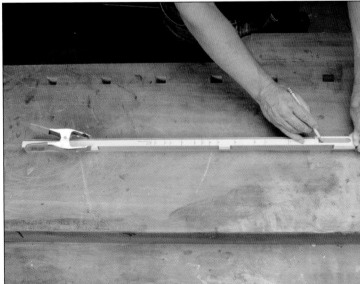

Using a story stick

Marking the Tuner Location

Now we need to mark the location for the tuners. Determine which side of the instrument you would like to place the tuners. Lay the tuner posts on top of the headstock, keeping them centered in the headstock slot. Draw a pencil line on both sides of the tuner posts. Turn the neck over and transfer a line down the sides of the instrument from the center of the tuner post location. Mark the location on the side of the headstock for the tuner posts with an awl. This will help to keep the drill bit from wandering when you drill the holes. It is important to drill these holes accurately in order to allow the tuner posts to turn freely in the hole. The measurement for the tuner posts might vary depending on the brand of mandolin tuners that you use. You will want to lay out the location carefully. It would be wise to practice this with a scrap piece before drilling the instrument. Keep in mind that the headstock will be angled, so you will want to keep the tuners parallel with the bottom of the headstock.

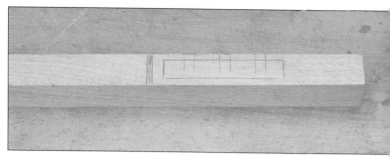

Tuner post locations

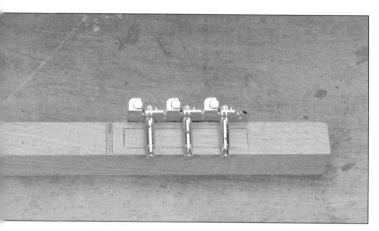

Centering the tuners on headstock

Squaring center of tuner posts down the side of the neck

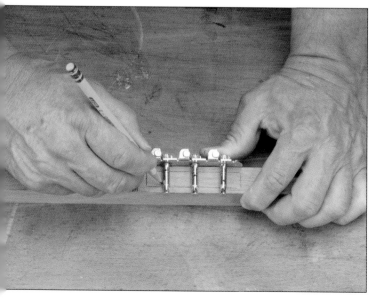

Marking tuner posts on both sides of post

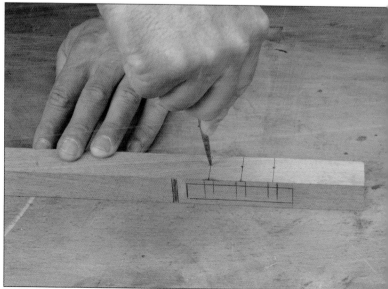

Marking post locations for drilling

19

Slotting for the Nut and the Top Notch

It is a good practice to notch the nut slot before laying out the fret slot locations since the fret slots need to be laid out very accurately. Having the nut slot located will ensure that the exact location of the front of the nut is established, which will be beneficial to laying out the fret slots. I will demonstrate cutting the slot on a table saw, however, if you do not have a table saw, you can cut this slot with a Japanese style handsaw and clean out the slot with a 1/8" chisel. For slotting with a table saw, first set the blade height to 1/8". Most combination table saw blades will produce a 1/8" wide slot. Use a miter gauge to hold the neck as you cut the slot across the neck. Since we have the table saw set, we will also cut a slot where the top meets the fingerboard.

Cutting slot for notch for top

Slots cut for nut and top

Setting blade height to 1/8"

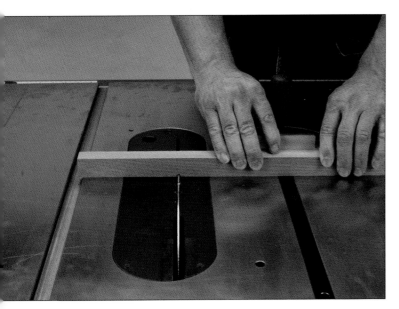

Cutting slot for nut

Marking Fret Slot Locations

Now that the nut slot is cut, we can mark the fret slot locations. We will cut the fret slots during the fretting process, but it is best to complete all layout steps at the same time. Use a ruler that is long enough to span the length of the fingerboard. Hold the "zero" line of the ruler at the front of the nut slot and tape the ruler to the fingerboard with low tack painter's tape. It is important to be accurate when marking the fret slots. If the fret slots are in the wrong location, it can cause certain notes of the instrument to sound out of tune. Use a digital caliper to measure the decimal dimension in conjunction with the ruler for the whole numbers. For example, our first fret location is 2.48" from the nut. Set the digital caliper to .48. Hold one side of the caliper jaw on the 2" mark while marking the fingerboard on the other side of the caliper. After all the fret slot locations are marked, use a square and a scriber, or marking knife, to score a line across the fingerboard. By scoring a line, you are creating a shallow groove that will help guide the saw while cutting the fret slots.

Fret Slot Dimensions from Face of Nut

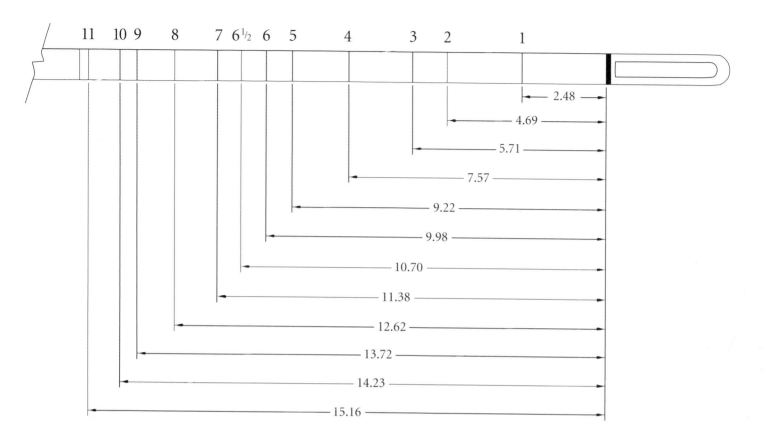

11	10 9	8	7 6½	6 5	4	3 2	1						

2.48
4.69
5.71
7.57
9.22
9.98
10.70
11.38
12.62
13.72
14.23
15.16

Fasten ruler to fingerboard

Scribing fret slot locations

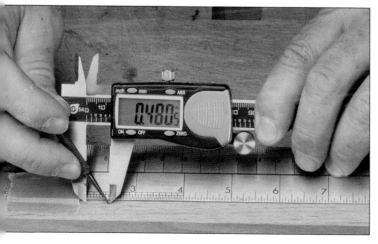

Marking fret slot locations with a digital caliper

Completed fret slot locations

All of the basic layout is now complete. Take some time to double check all dimensions. Stop and take a deep breath and admire your work to this point. You are off to a good start!

Understanding Fret Layout

If you build an instrument with a different string length (or scale length) than the one shown here, you will need to do the math to figure out the fret placement. The basic rule for fret placement is that when you shorten the string by 1/18, it raises the sound one semi-tone. This is called the rule of 18. The actual number used to calculate fret placement is 17.81715.

Our pickin' stick has a string length of 22.75". To find the location of the first fret (based on all half notes), divide the string length (22.75") by 17.81715, which results in 1.28". This would be the location of the first fret from the nut if we were using all half notes as in a guitar. Since we will not be using the first half step, we will not use this dimension except to calculate the location of the next fret.

To find the location of the second half step (or the first fret of the pickin' stick, subtract the first half step dimension from the overall string length (22.75" − 1.28" = 21.47"). This will be the dimension from the first half note to the saddle. Now divide the remainder by 17.81715 (21.47" / 17.81715" = 1.20"). This will be the location of the second half note from the first half note. Add the first two half notes to calculate the location of the first fret (the first whole note) of the pickin' stick from the nut (2.48").

So to figure all of the fret locations on the pickin' stick, you will first need to find the location of all of the half notes as if it were for a guitar. The chart below shows the dimensions of all of the half notes and the location of the pickin' stick frets to help understand the relationship between the two. The pickin' stick fingerboard is basically just like a guitar fingerboard with the "in between" notes taken away.

Guitar Fret (Half Notes)	Pickin' Stick Frets (Whole and Half Notes)	Dimension from Nut
1		1.27
2	1	2.48
3		3.62
4	2	4.69
5	3	5.71
6		6.67
7	4	7.57
8		8.42
9	5	9.22
10	6	9.98
11	6.5	10.7
12	7	11.38
13		12.02
14	8	12.62
15		13.19
16	9	13.72
17	10	14.23

The 6.5 Fret

You might be wondering what the 6.5 fret is all about. The 6.5 fret is a chromatic fret, which allows a half step within the diatonic scale. This fret placement is not part of the major scale. With the addition of this fret, you have an increased range to allow you to play notes that do not fall within the major scale.

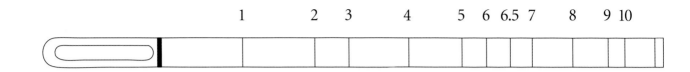

Pickin' Stick Fingerboard - Combination of Half Notes and Whole Notes

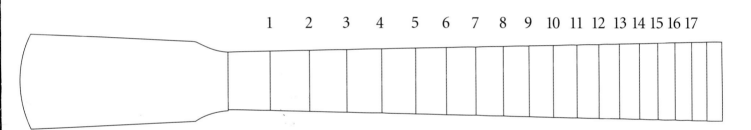

Guitar Fingerboard - All Half Notes

Comparing pickin' stick fret placement to a guitar's

Chapter 6
Shaping the Ends of the Neck

Drilling the Headstock

We now need to excavate the headstock to allow the strings to be connected to the tuners. You can use a chisel, a hand drill, a hollow chisel mortiser, or a drill press. I prefer to use a doweling jig in conjunction with a drill press. Since the sides of the headstock will end up being only 3/16" thick, it would be easy to get the slot off center when doing it by hand.

The doweling jig keeps the slot centered and makes the process much easier. Chuck a 3/8" drill bit in the drill press. Align the leading hole in the dowel jig with one of the lines laid out for the headstock. Drill a series of holes until you have drilled the full length of the headstock slot. Turn the neck on its side and drill the holes for the tuners using a 1/4" bit. If you are building multiple instruments, you might want to take the time to make a drilling template for the tuners.

Drilling for tuner posts

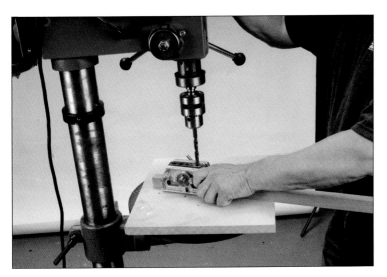

Drilling out headstock slot with doweling jig

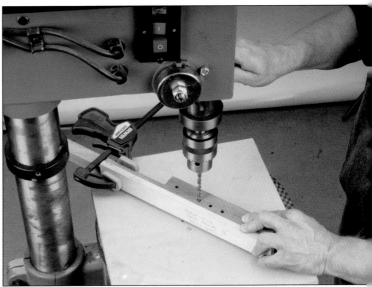

Using a template to drill tuner posts

Cleaning Out the Headstock Slot

Clean out the headstock by hand using a sharp chisel and flat sanding blocks. Place the neck in a vice and carefully pare the sides of the slot to the layout line. Sand the insides of the slot using a 1/4" x 1" sanding block.

A router template makes a nice job of this process. Clamp the neck firmly to the jig to avoid chatter and tear out. You will need a long 1/4" tracing router bit. Make several passes with the router for the cleanest cut.

Routing headstock slot

Cleaning headstock slot with a paring chisel

Headstock routing jig

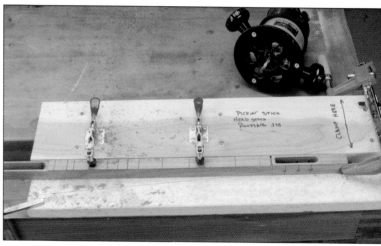

Completed headstock routing

Cutting the Sides for the Sound Box

The sides for the sound box are formed from cuts in the stick and you will need to cut those before shaping the neck and headstock. Since the top is 1/8" thick, we will first need to cut the end of the neck 1/8" in order to keep the top flush with the fingerboard. Make sure you are cutting on the same side as the fingerboard. You can use a table saw or a band saw to do this. Stop this cut at the notch for the top. When using a table saw you will need to use a chisel to clean up the end of the cut.

Before cutting the sides, drill a 5/8" relief hole at the end of the cut. The location of this hole is about 3/4" from the very last fret slot mark. Keep it centered in the width of the neck. To cut the sides, set up a fence on the band saw 1/8" from the blade. Cut both sides of the sound box, stopping at the relief hole. Remove the piece from the center and discard.

Neck clamped in place for routing

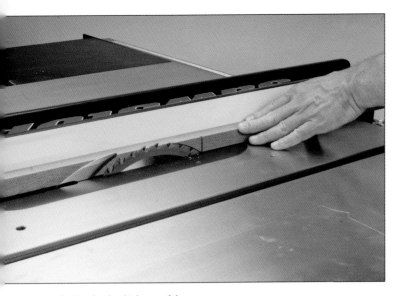

Cutting for the thickness of the top

Cleaning out the cut for the top

Drilling a 5/8" relief hole

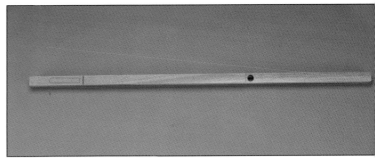

Neck after drilling relief hole

Cutting the sides of the sound box

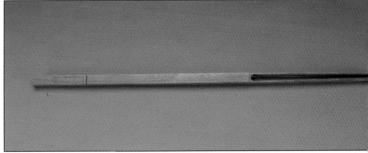

Neck after cutting sides of the sound box

Rounding Over the Back of the Neck

Round over the back of the neck using a router with a 1/2" router bit. Stop the rout before you get to the sides for the sound box and before you reach the nut. Make a mark on both sides of the neck at the last fret location. Use this as a visual reference to stop the router. Make a similar mark at the front edge of the nut. Do not sand the back of the neck until the back and top are glued in place.

Marking location to stop route for back of neck

Rounding over back of neck with 1/2" round over bit

The end of the route looks like this by the sound box

The end of the route looks like this by the nut

Final Cutting of the Headstock

The headstock will now need to be cut to length. You can leave this as long or as short as you like. You can cut out a shape or carve it or just round over the end. This is an opportunity to use your creativity. For this project, we will measure 3/4" from the end of the headstock slot and round the end. After it is cut to length, we need to cut the headstock at an angle. This makes it easier to reach the tuner pegs and gives it a more elegant design. Make a mark 1/4" down the side of the headstock. Place a straight edge from this mark to the opposite end of the headstock slot. Draw a line at this angle. Cut the top of the headstock and sand smooth with a sanding block. Finish by rounding over the end of the headstock.

Mark and cut the end of the headstock to length

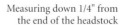

Measuring down 1/4" from the end of the headstock

Placing straightedge at top of headstock slot

Sanding angle on headstock

Marking the angle with the straightedge

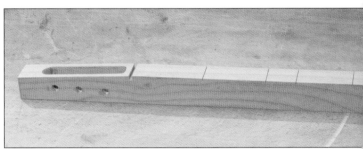

Headstock before final shaping

Cutting headstock angle

Rounding over end of headstock

Final Shaping of the Headstock

The headstock needs to be shaped to allow the strings to follow from the nut to the tuners without touching the sides of the headstock slot. Begin with a round rasp to file at an angle towards the nut slot. Next, file the front edge, rounding it over so that the radius is leading up to the nut slot. Be careful not to disturb the nut slot. Now file the inside and outside edges of the nut slot until there are no sharp edges. Finish up with 80-grit sandpaper on all sides.

Filing the edges to a create clear path for the strings

Filing the corners of the headstock slot

Rounding over top end of headstock edge

Ramping the front of the headstock slot

Rounding over inside edges of headstock with a file

29

Rounding over inside edges of headstock with sandpaper

Sanding corners of headstock

Filing the outside edges on the back of the headstock

Turn the neck over and blend the radius on the back of the neck into the headstock using a half-round file. Round over the inside and outside edges of the headstock slot with files and sandpaper.

The goal in shaping the headstock and the neck is to make the parts look like they blend together. The point where the router stopped should not be visible, instead it should look like it flows gracefully from one component to the next. Rub your hand back and forth across these areas without looking at them. If you feel any edges, go back with sandpaper and smooth them out.

We are now ready to begin assembling the pickin' stick.

Filing the inside edges on the back of the headstock

Blending radius on the back of the neck with the headstock

Rounding over the end of the headstock slot

30

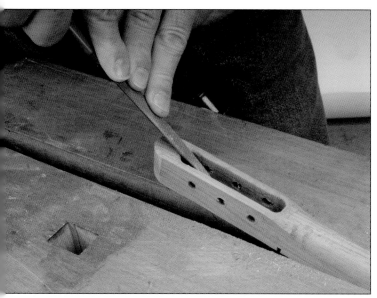

Rounding over the top end of the headstock slot

Sanding the top end of the headstock

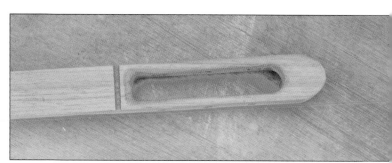

The fingerboard side of the shaped headstock

Sanding the outside edges

The back side of the shaped headstock

Chapter 7
Making the End Block

The end block helps define the shape of the sound box. The shape of it is not important. If you prefer, you can make the end block flat rather than cut at a radius. You can use this as an opportunity to show off your creativity. For our pickin' stick, we are using a 3 1/2" radius on the end block.

While the shape of the end block is not important, the thickness is. It must be exactly the same thickness as the width of the sides. We started out with a neck that was 1 1/16" thick. Since the top is 1/8" thick, we cut the top of the neck down 1/8" so that the top of the sound box will be the same height as the fingerboard. This means that our end block needs to be 15/16" thick. If your neck is not 1 1/16" thick, you will need to adjust the thickness of the end block accordingly.

Marking the length of the end block

Marking a 14-degree angle

Steps for Making the End Block

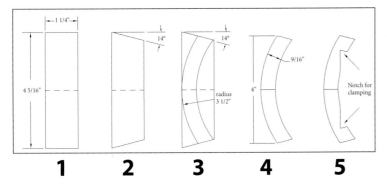

1   2   3   4   5

Marking the center line

Laying Out the End Block

Taking the 15/16" x 1 1/4" material, measure 4 5/16" from one end and cut the end block blank to length. Draw a 14-degree angle on both ends. Cut the angles with a miter saw or table saw. If you do not have a power saw, this angle can easily be cut by hand with a Japanese style pull saw. Make sure you draw a center line at this point. It is important to draw it dark enough so it will not wear off. This will serve as a reference mark for several future steps. Draw the radius on the side that will be the outside of the instrument. You are now ready to cut out the end block.

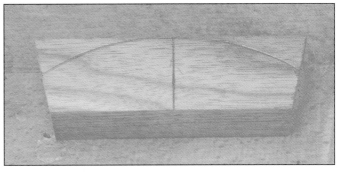

The end block lines laid out

Cutting the End Block

Cut the outside radius of the end block. Sand this with a disc sander or sanding block so it has a smooth surface. Now that this radius has been cut, the end block is 4" in width from the long points. This is our target dimension for the finished end block.

The cuts on the inside of the end block do not have to be perfect. Cut the inside radius first. Now cut a notch on the inside on both ends about 3/8" from the end. This notch will give the clamps a surface to clamp to when gluing the sides to the end block.

Keep in mind that we want to keep the instrument as light as possible to allow the sound box to vibrate as much as possible. So, do not be afraid to remove material from the inside. The finished end block should be about 1/2" to 9/16" wide when completed.

Gluing the End Block to the Sides

Before gluing the end block to the sides, take the time to dry fit the parts. Gently spread the sides while sliding the end block in place. The outside of the end block should line up with the marks made during the layout process. Did you remember to transfer this mark down the sides of the neck before you cut out for the top? If not, you have cut off your layout mark and will need to mark it again. Measure down from the notch where the top meets the fingerboard and make a mark at 9 3/4".

Cutting the radius

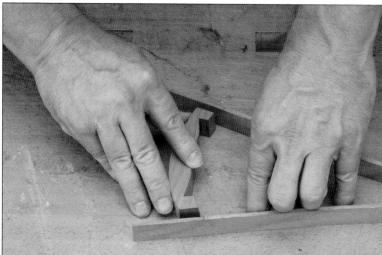

Dry fitting the end block to the sides

End block before and after cutting

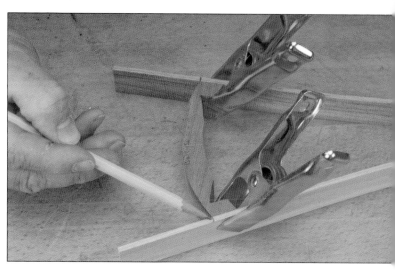

Reference marks for lining up the end block

You are now ready to glue the end block in place. Apply some Titebond® glue to the ends and work the glue into the grain of the wood. Since we are gluing end grain, make sure that there are no dry spots after you have spread the glue. Place the neck on a flat surface and gently spread the sides as you did when dry fitting. Check to make sure that the outside corner of the end block lines up with the marks on the sides. Make sure the end block is flush with the sides.

Apply two spring clamps on top. Turn it over and apply two more spring clamps. Allow it to dry for at least an hour.

After the end block is dry, remove the clamps and trim the sides to the end block. Do not sand this joint at this time. This corner will be sanded all together once the top and back are glued in place. As a final step, sand the top of the sides flush with the end block. This will provide a perfect gluing surface for the top and back.

Applying glue to the end block

Clamping the end block to the sides

Positioning the end block

Trimming the sides to the end block

Sanding the sides flush with the end block

Chapter 8
Closing the Sound Box

We are now ready to close the sound box. This consists of cutting out the top and back and gluing them onto the sides. Glue the back and top at separate times. This makes the glue clean up easier and makes alignment of the plates easier.

Cutting Out the Back

Before gluing, cut out the back and top close to the final profile. Use a template to trace the pattern to the back. Make the back long enough to extend past the area where we stopped the round over of the back of the neck. When cutting the profile, do not cut to the line, but leave about 1/4" of material on the outside of the lines. The overhang will be trimmed flush with the sides after the back and top are glued in place.

Cutting out the back profile

Tracing the sound box profile on the back

Keeping it Centered

It is critical at this juncture to maintain the center line of the pickin' stick. To accomplish this, make sure you transfer the center line mark on the end block down the full thickness of the end. Make a dark mark so it is readily visible. Use a glue board to keep all parts aligned during the clamping process. It should be long enough to set the full length of the instrument on. Draw a dark line down the center of the length of the board. Measure one half the width of the neck (7/16") from the center line and make a mark. Glue a couple of small blocks at this location. These blocks will serve as stop blocks and hold the neck during the clamping process.

Center line marked on end block

Glue board

Gluing on the Back

Before applying glue to any surfaces, gather all of the tools and parts you will need for the glue up process. Make sure you have enough clamps nearby so that you will not need to hunt for clamps while the glue is quickly drying. It is a good idea to dry fit the parts to ensure that everything lines up before applying glue.

Glue the edges of the sides and the end block. Use enough glue to cover the surfaces, but not so much that glue is running down the surface of the instrument. A little glue squeeze out is desirable and indicates that there are no dry spots. Place the back on the glue board. Position the neck on the glue board and clamp in place. Be sure to line up the center line on the end block with the center line on the clamping board. Glue the end block down first to keep the center lines established. Now continue clamping around the rest of the sound box.

Applying glue to the sides

Positioning the neck and back in place

Lining up the center line on the glue board

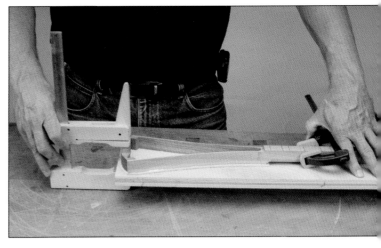

Clamping the end block in place

Applying remaining clamps

All clamps in place

Cutting Out the Top

Using the same template that you used for the back, trace the sound box outline on the top. Draw a center line on the side that will be exposed. Measure 4 1/2" from where the end of the sound box meets the finger board. This is the center of the sound hole. Mark this point with an awl. Using an awl will keep the drill bit from wandering while drilling. Cut out the top in the same way you did for the back, cutting about 1/4" outside the lines, with the exception of the end that joins with the fingerboard. Cut this end on the line and sand it to make a seamless fit. Using a flat bottom bit, drill a 3/4" hole for the sound hole. Drill from the side that will be exposed so that any tear out will not be visible.

Marking the sound hole with an awl

Tracing the top profile

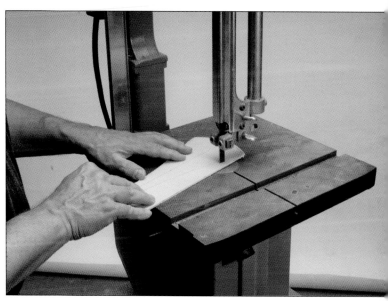

Completed layout for top

Drawing center line on top

Cutting out the top profile

Locating the sound hole

Drilling the sound hole

Preparation for Gluing

Before gluing the top on, take the time to clean up any glue squeeze out on the inside of the sound box. If you want to write your signature inside or apply a label, this is the time to do it. Dry fit the top to make sure all joints are tight and that the sound hole is centered. Check the joint where the fingerboard and the soundboard meet. Make a center line mark at the end of the fingerboard to help keep the top aligned.

Applying a label

Dry fitting the top

Marking the center line on the fingerboard

Gluing the Top

Apply glue to the sides as you did when gluing the back. Clamp the end next to the finger board first to make sure that you have a good fit at the joint. Next, glue the end block, keeping the center lines lined up. Now continue clamping around the sound box.

Your pickin' stick is really starting to take shape. Take some time to stand back and admire your work.

Applying glue to the sides

Aligning the center lines at the fingerboard

Applying the remaining clamps

Aligning the center lines at the end block

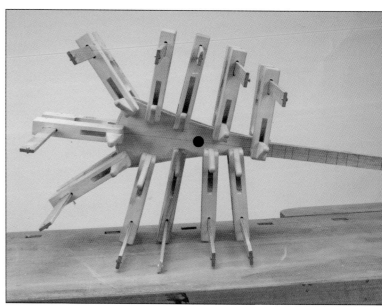

All clamps in place

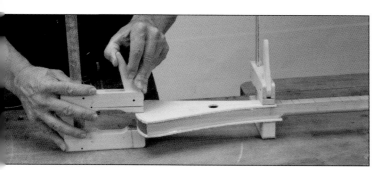

Clamping the end block

Chapter 9
Final Shaping of the Sound Box

We have one task left to do before we can consider the assembly process complete, and that is to trim the top and back to the sides and give the sound box its final shape.

Trimming the top and back with a router

Sanding the edges of the sound box

Trimming the Top and Back

Using a router with a flush trim bit, trim the overhang of the top and back flush with the sides and end of the instrument. If you don't have a router, this can be done with a chisel and sanding block. Do not concern yourself with the outside corners of the end block at this point, as they will be shaped later. Sand the sides with a radius sanding block until you can no longer feel where the back or top meet the sides.

Final Shaping of the Back

We now need to blend the back of the sound box with the radius of the back of the neck. To do this we will use a rasp, a file, and a round sanding block. Clamp the neck securely in a vice. Use a course half-round rasp to start, knocking off the square edges. Rasp the back down until it begins to blend with the neck. When you reach this point, use a finer half-round file to smooth it out and bring it to its final shape. Now use a round sanding block and hand sand to clean up all edges. You want this area to blend well with no sharp edges. When you run your fingers over this area, you should not be able to feel where the back ends and the neck begins.

Blending the back with the neck

Final shaping with a half-round file

Final shaping with a sanding block

Shaping the corners with a disc sander

Final sanding

Sanding the top flush with the fingerboard

Final Touches

It is time to round the outside corners of the sound box. A disc sander is ideal for this, but this can be done with a sanding block as well. Sand the corners round until the sides blend with the end block.

Now sand the top flush with the fingerboard using a flat sanding block. Ease all remaining square edges with 120-grit sandpaper.

There is one final detail in the shaping process. We need to visualize where the strings will pass over the end of the instrument to attach to the end pins. To minimize the strings gouging into the top, file a "ramp" over the end to give the string path a more gradual transition. You may choose to place a small piece of felt or leather under the strings to help protect the top.

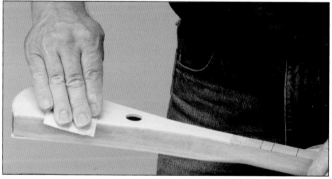
Easing the edges of the top

Filing a ramp for the strings

41

Chapter 10
Installing Frets

Installing the frets is the last step before stringing the instrument. The fret locations were marked during the layout process. The fret slots can be cut at any time, however, you might find it easiest to cut them before gluing in the end block so that it fits into a bench vice easier.

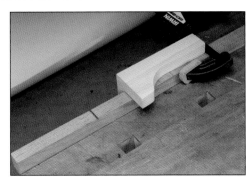

Jig for cutting fret slots

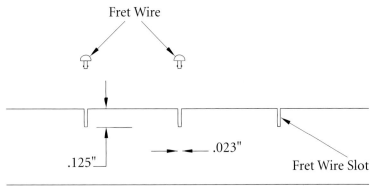

Fret Wire

.125"   .023"

Fret Wire Slot

Side View of Neck and Fingerboard

Fret slot dimensions

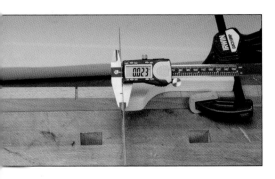

Measuring saw blade thickness (.023")

Cutting the Fret Slots

It is important to keep the fret slots square with the sides of the neck. While you can accomplish this by cutting free hand, making a simple jig will assure that you are cutting straight. Make the jig in such a way that you can clamp it to the neck to keep it from moving. The fret slots need to be .023" wide and 1/8" deep to accommodate common fret wire sizes. If the fret slot is too narrow, it will cause the neck to bow, making the instrument difficult to set up correctly. Measure your saw blade with a caliper to make sure it will cut the appropriate slot. Ride the side of the blade against the fence of the cutting jig and cut a straight kerf about 1/8" deep. The slot will be a little bit deeper than the tang of the fret, which is what we want. We don't want the tang to bottom out on the bottom of the cut or the fret will not sit properly.

Cutting fret slots

Completed fret slotting

Fingerboard Preparation

Sand the fingerboard with a flat sanding block. Sand with 120-, 220- and 320-grit to get a fine, smooth feeling fingerboard. Clean out the fret slots with a fine blade or knife. Ease the edges of the fingerboard so that you will not feel any sharp edges. Filing the fret slots lightly with a triangle file will assist in the installation of the fret slots. Cut all of the fret wire to length using a wire cutter, leaving about 1/4" of overhang on both sides of the fingerboard.

Filing the fret slots with a triangular file

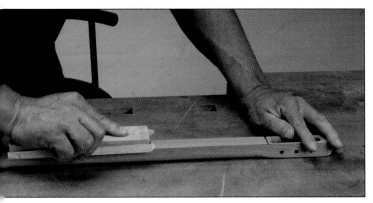

Final sanding of fingerboard

Cleaning out fret slots

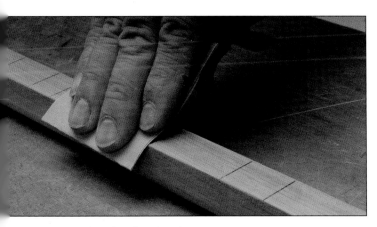

Easing the edges of the fingerboard

Cutting fret wire to length

43

Fret Wire Installation

Although you can hammer in the frets with the neck sitting flat on the workbench, it is a good idea to put something underneath the area where the fret is being installed to absorb the hammer blows. A bag of shot is ideal, but a bag of sand works as well.

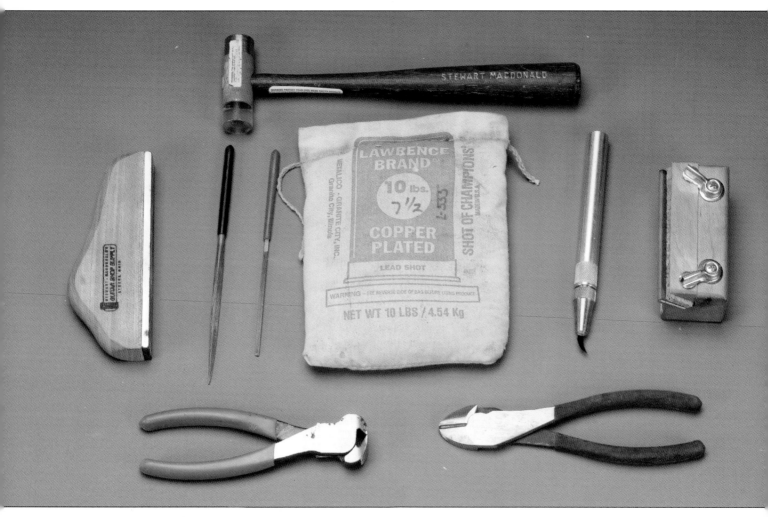

Fretting tools

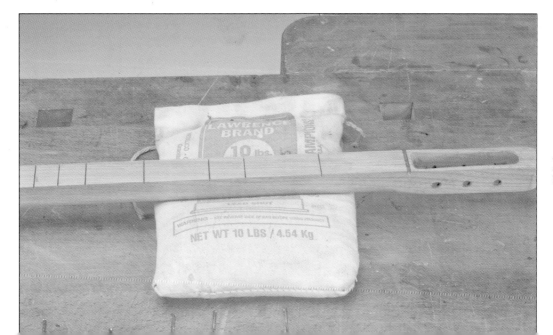

A Bag of shot to absorb the hammer blows

We are now ready to install the frets. You will need a small hammer that will not damage the fret wire to hammer the frets into the fingerboard. Force some Titebond® glue down into the fret slots. By using this water-based glue, the cells of the wood will swell around the barbs of the fret tang, essentially locking them into place. Although you can install fret wire without glue, the gluing method will yield better results. It is important be neat with the glue. Wipe off the excess immediately so that it will not show through the finish.

Place a pre-cut fret wire and hold it in place while tapping one end in place to secure it. Now hammer across the fret wire until the shoulders of the fret wire are seated against the fingerboard. Do not hammer too hard or too many times, as this can loosen the fret wire. Hammering once or twice across the fret wire will be sufficient. After all the fret wire is installed, sight down the fingerboard to check for any frets that might not be seated. If you notice any frets that are not seated, tap them down into place. If you find any that will not stay down, clamp it down until the glue has dried.

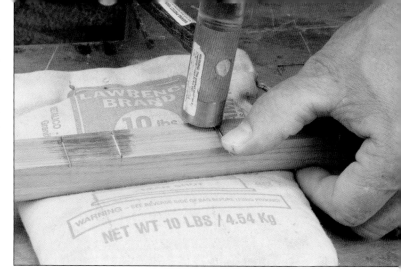
Getting the fret started in the slot

Gluing the fret slots

Hammering frets into place

Wiping off excess glue

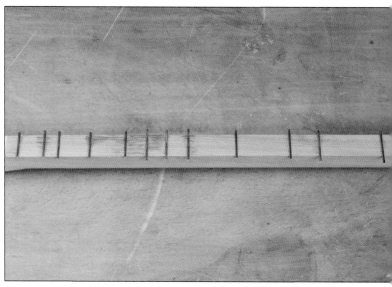
All frets installed

Checking to make sure all frets are seated

Trimming the Frets

Now that the frets are all installed, it is time to trim them flush with the fingerboard and file them smooth so that your fingers will glide over them easily without feeling any sharp edges. Start by trimming the ends of the fret wire flush with the fingerboard. Use end cutting pliers that have the end ground flush so that it will trim the frets as close as possible.

Cutting frets flush with the fingerboard

All frets cut

Turn the pickin' stick on edge and file the ends of the fret wire flush with the fingerboard. You will be able to hear the file fall silent when the fret ends are flush with the neck. Next, file the ends back to about a 30-degree bevel. You can use a file made for this purpose, or simply use a regular file and bevel each fret wire separately. Now use a small file to round over the sharp edges. The file shown here has the teeth ground off on the bottom so that it will not damage the fingerboard.

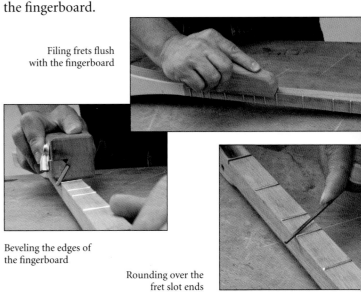

Filing frets flush with the fingerboard

Beveling the edges of the fingerboard

Rounding over the fret slot ends

Filling the Fret End Slots

Our fret slots were cut deeper than the tang of the fret wire so that the fret would not bottom out in the slot. We want to fill these slots so that they will not be visible after finishing. To do this, fill the slots with sawdust by sanding the edges with 220-grit sandpaper until the slots are full. Place a dab of thin super glue over each fret slot. Keep a rag handy to catch any excess. After the glue has dried a little bit, sand it once again until you can see no glue residue. The fret slots will now be practically invisible.

We are getting close to being able to string our instrument. But first we need to install the nut, saddle, and tuners.

Filling fret end slots by sanding

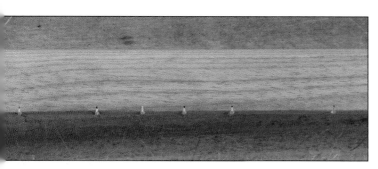

Fret ends slots before filling

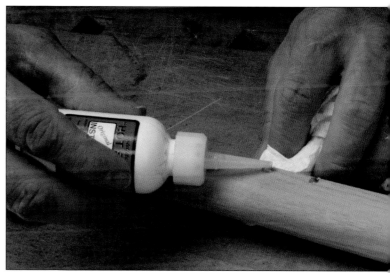

Gluing slot ends with thin super glue

Chapter 11
Preparing the Nut and Saddle

Making the Nut

We are now ready to install the nut and tuners as well as prepare the saddle in preparation for stringing the pickin' stick. We will begin with the nut. We will first fit the nut to the slot, and then establish the height of the nut above the fingerboard. The nut should measure 1/8" thick, 1/4" wide, and 1 1/4" long. These dimensions will allow for trimming to the final dimensions.

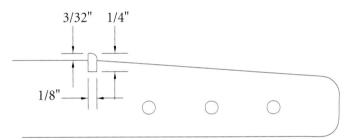

Nut Detail

Fitting the Nut

The nut should be "finger tight," meaning that you should be able to press it in and remove it without the use of tools. To start, the nut should not quite fit into the slot so that you can fit it perfectly. To do this, lay it on its side on a sanding block with 220-grit sandpaper. Sand a few strokes and check the fit. Repeat this until it will fit all the way down into the slot. Be careful that you do not sand too much or the nut will be too loose.

Thinning the nut to fit

Once the nut is seated all the way down in the slot, take a measurement from the top of the fingerboard to the top of the nut. This dimension should be about 3/32". If your measurement is more than 3/32" you will need to sand or file from the top of the nut until you reach this dimension. If your measurement is less than 3/32" you should make a new nut. Once you are satisfied with the fit of the nut, shape the back side of the nut by rounding it over with a file or sandpaper. Make sure that you do not disturb the front edge of the nut (the edge facing the sound box), as we want a clean straight line where the string breaks over the top of it.

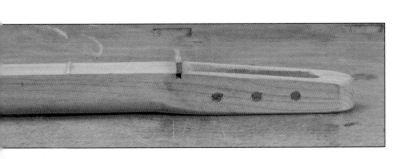

Checking the fit of the nut in the nut slot

The nut seated in the nut slot

Shaping the back of the nut, the side facing the headstock

Place a little glue on the bottom of the nut and clamp it into place. Once the glue has dried, trim the sides of the nut flush with the neck. Sand flush with 220-grit sandpaper.

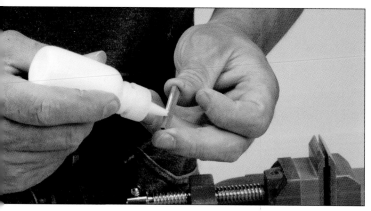

Gluing the bottom of the nut

Clamping the nut

Cutting the nut flush with the neck

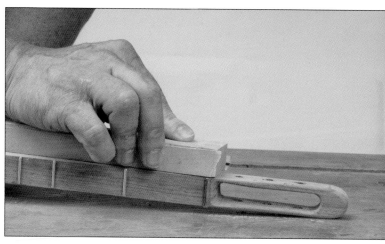

Sanding the nut flush with the neck

Making the Saddle

The saddle is placed in a specific location below the sound hole and defines the length of the string, giving it the correct intonation. We will review exactly where it is located when we discuss final set up procedures. For now, we need to prepare the saddle so that it is ready when we string the instrument. The angle can be difficult and dangerous to cut since it is such a small piece, so cut the saddle to the correct width and height then clamp it in a vice and shape the angle with a block plane. You could also hold it down using double stick tape.

Approximate location for the saddle

Saddle Dimensions

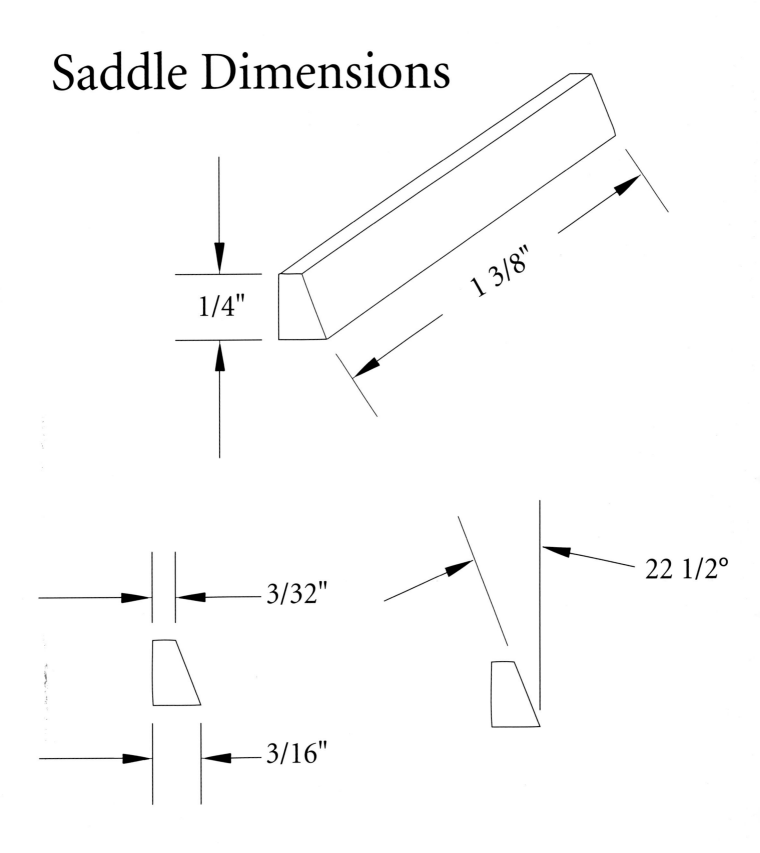

1/4"

1 3/8"

3/32"

3/16"

22 1/2°

Chapter 12
Installing the Tuners and End Pins

Preparing the Tuners

The tuners we will be using for the pickin' stick are actually mandolin tuners. If you prefer, you can also use violin pegs in place of mandolin tuners. A mandolin has eight strings with four strings on each side of the headstock. Each set of tuners has 4 tuning shafts. We will be using one side of a set of two tuners. However, we will need to modify the tuners to fit the three strings of the pickin' stick.

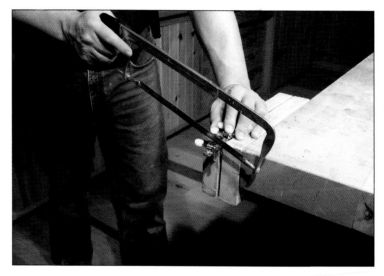

Cutting mandolin tuner to length

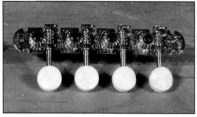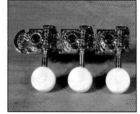

Mandolin tuners before (left) and after (right) cutting

We need to cut off one of the tuner posts from the tuners. Hold the tuners up near the headstock to determine which end you want to cut off. It does not matter if the tuner knobs turn up or down, or which side of the headstock they are installed. Cut the tuning shaft off with a hacksaw and polish the cut end with fine wet or dry sandpaper or emery cloth.

Mandolin tuner after cutting

Determining which end to cut

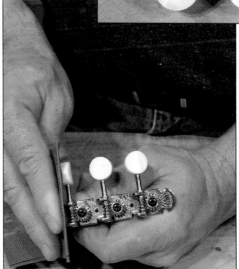

Polishing the end of the tuner

Place the tuners into the headstock. We will need to mark the holes in the tuner shafts for the strings to pass through. Use a marker to mark each shaft for the string location in a manner that will keep the string path from the nut to the tuner shaft as straight as possible. The tuner post for the middle string will be marked on the middle tuner post in the middle of the headstock slot and so on.

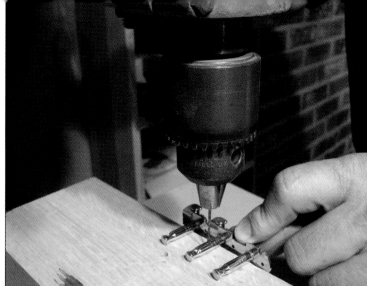

Drilling string holes

We are now ready to install the tuners. Fasten the tuners to the headstock using #2 x 1/4" screws. The screws that come with the tuners will be too long for the headstock. Be sure to drill a test hole in a piece of scrap wood and make sure the hole is the right size for the screw. The screws do not need to be real tight, so make sure the hole size will allow you to turn the screw in without much effort.

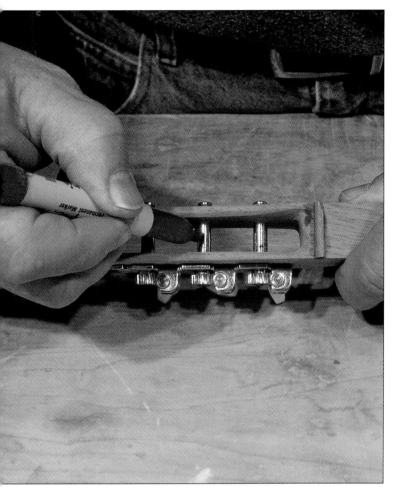

Marking location of string holes on tuner posts

Use a center punch to mark the hole location and to keep the drill bit from wandering. Set the tuner shafts on a block of wood and drill a 1/16" hole in each one.

Installing tuners with screws

Starting hole with center punch

Marking the End Pin Locations

The end pins hold the looped end of the strings. Their location is important in that they help keep the strings in line with the fingerboard. To keep the strings lined up, we need to find the center line of the instrument. Make a mark at the center where the fingerboard and top join together, as well as the center of the nut. Using a long straightedge, make a center line mark at the end block. This will be the location of the middle end pin. The other two end pins should match the dimensions of the string space at the nut.

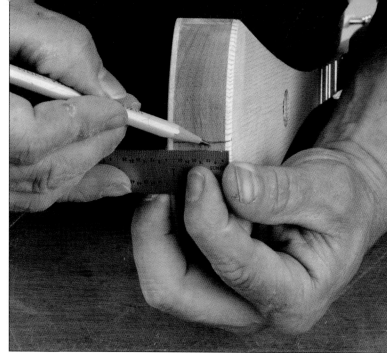

Marking the center end pin location

Marking the center line

On the end block measure down about 3/8" to 1/2" from the top to mark the end pin locations. They can all be the same height or you can stagger them, whichever you prefer. Make a mark with an awl to keep the drill bit from wandering. Drill into the end block for the pins with a drill bit size that will hold the end pins, yet allow you to pull them out later for finishing. Hold the drill at a slight angle so the pins are angled slightly downward. This will keep the strings from pulling off of the end pins. The holes should be sized so that you can tap them in lightly but still be loose enough to pull out with a pair of pliers. If the pins are left in, it will make the finishing process more difficult.

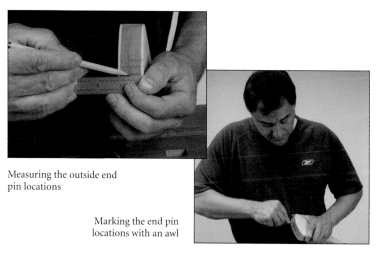

Measuring the outside end pin locations

Marking the center line on the end block

Marking the end pin locations with an awl

Drilling holes for end pins

Chapter 13
Stringing and Final Set Up

The moment has nearly arrived when you can finally string your instrument and hear it sing for the first time. This is a very exciting moment. The fruits of your labor are about to pay off. There are just a few steps to complete before we can install the strings.

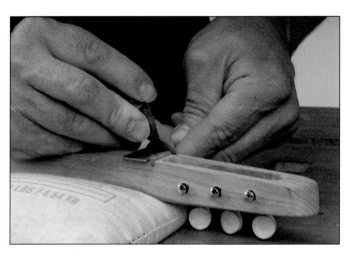

Marking string locations on the nut

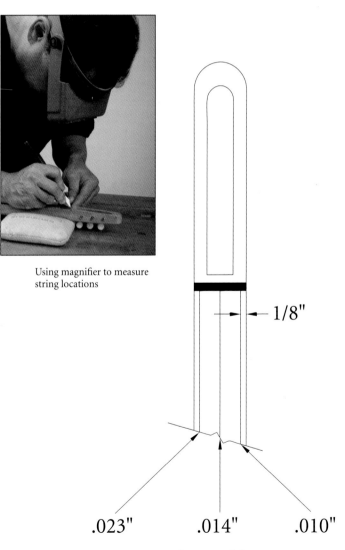

Using magnifier to measure string locations

.023"   .014"   .010"

String Sizes
(Use Mandolin String Set)

Slotting the Nut

Slotting the nut requires careful measuring and filing. Do not rush through this process or you will likely need to rework the nut. The goal is to keep the strings an equal distance apart and the strings at the correct height. Use a pair of magnifiers when measuring, even if you think you have good eyesight. This can make a big difference in the accuracy of your layout lines.

Use a marking knife when marking the string locations. A marking knife will give a slight groove, which will help the nut file stay on the correct mark. It is very easy to wander from a pencil mark and end up with nut slot that is off. Measure 1/8" from the end of both sides of the nut and make a mark. Now measure and make a mark exactly half way between the outside marks.

The nut needs to be slotted to fit the size of the string that will be passing through it. If the slot is too large, it can cause the string to rattle. If the slot it to small, the string will catch in the nut slot when you try to bring the instrument into tune. I generally try to make the slot just a few thousandths larger than the string, which gives it just enough room to move freely.

Gauged nut files made specifically for this task are the best tools of choice for filing the string slots. Not only are they sized for various string sizes, but they also have a round shape to match the profile of the strings. If you do not have access to a set of nut files, you can use a small needle file or a small saw.

The depth of the slot should only be about 1/32" at this point. We will adjust it to its final depth after the strings are on. When filing these slots, the file should be aimed towards the hole that the string will be going through. Keep the file slanted slightly downward towards the tuner shaft.

Hooking a string on the end pin

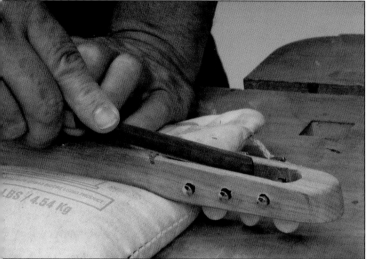

Filing slots in the nut for strings

Inserting the end of the string into the tuner shaft

Stringing Up

Mandolin strings are used for the pickin' stick since they have a loop on the end of them. Purchase a light gauge set which will typically give you eight strings of two diameters each: .010 and .014, which are plain strings (unwound) and .023 and .034, which have a winding around a plain core. We will not use the .034 gauge so it is best to set it aside so that you will not install it accidentally.

Install the two outside strings first. Hook the loop end over the appropriate end pin. If you have trouble keeping it on the end pin, put some tape over it to hold it in place until the string tension holds it in place. Turn the tuners so all of the holes are visible. Put the string through the hole and turn the tuners so that the string is winding over the top of the tuner shaft. Leave enough slack in the string so that the string will wind around the shaft a couple of times to prevent it from slipping. At this point, keep the strings fairly loose so you can slip the saddle underneath the strings.

String installation method

All strings installed

55

Installing the Saddle

The saddle will not be glued in place until after the finish is applied. Gluing is not really necessary as the string tension will hold it in place. However, if it has a tendency to slide to one side, a drop or two of instant glue after finish will keep it in place. For now, lift up on the strings and place the saddle underneath them in the approximate saddle location. Tighten the strings just enough to keep the saddle from moving.

and thinner. The same thing happens to the instrument strings when you press them down on the fretboard. For this reason we need to adjust the saddle back about 1/16" to account for the lengthening of the string. You will notice that the saddle is also canted to one side. This angle compensates for the larger strings which will stretch more than the smaller strings.

Use a long ruler to measure the saddle position. Before measuring, check to verify that the saddle is centered on the center line. When measuring for the saddle location, double check to make sure that you are measuring from the face of the nut. Measure 22 3/4" from the nut to the front edge of the top of the saddle for the .010 string. Measure 22 7/8" from the nut to the top edge of the saddle for the .023 string. Check these measurements several times to make sure that one side has not shifted.

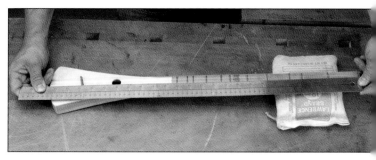

Measuring from nut to saddle for the first string

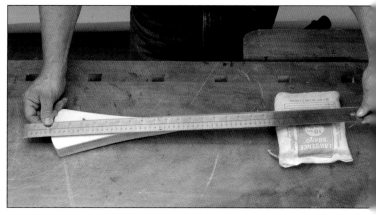

Measuring from nut to saddle on third string

Placing saddle into position

Saddle Compensation

The saddle location is based on the scale length (sometimes referred to as string length [22 3/4"]) of the instrument, from which the fret locations were calculated. If we place the saddle at this dimension however, it would sound out of tune when you play. Picture the strings as you would a rubber band. If you pull on the rubber band it gets longer

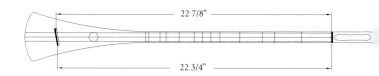

Dimensions from Nut to Saddle

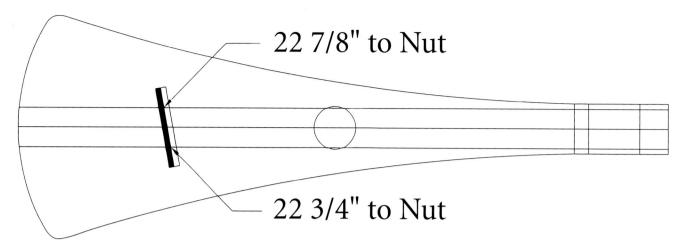

22 7/8" to Nut

22 3/4" to Nut

Saddle location

Before doing anything else, make a pencil mark at the front edge of the saddle and one of the ends. Position the two outside strings so that the string is running perfectly parallel with the edge of the fingerboard. Hold the string in place while you make a pencil mark on both sides of the strings on the saddle. Once both outside strings are marked, move the center string exactly in the center and make a mark on both sides of this string. File a shallow slot with the appropriate nut file to keep the string in line. These slots will be adjusted after the strings have been tuned to pitch.

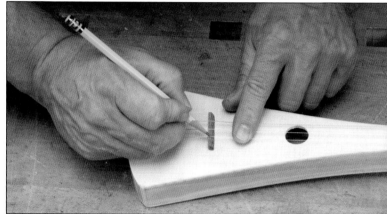

Marking both sides of strings on saddle

Marking front of saddle

Marking end of saddle

Slotting saddle for strings

57

Adjusting String Height

After the strings are tuned to pitch, measure the space between the fret wire and the bottom of the string at the first and tenth frets. Check and adjust the nut first. This space at the first fret should measure about 3/64" to 2/32". If the string is higher than this measurement, loosen the string, pull the string out of the nut slot, and file it down a little more. File a little bit at a time and check the measurement frequently. If the string slot is too low, you can pack some fine sanding dust into the nut slot and put a drop of thin super glue on it. After the glue has dried you can re-cut the nut slot.

The dimension from the top of the fret to the bottom of the string at the tenth fret should measure 4/32" to 5/32". If the string is higher than this measurement, make the adjustment at the saddle. Pull the string out of the saddle slot and file it down as you did on the nut.

Enjoy the moment as you reflect on all that you have accomplished to get to this point.

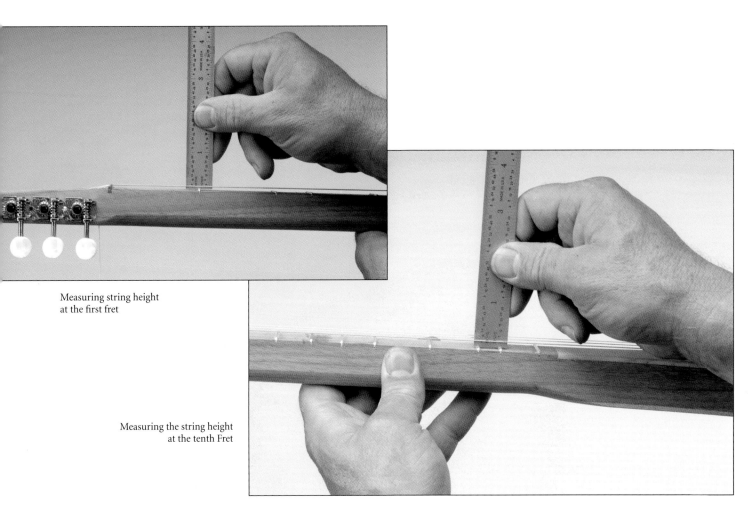

Measuring string height
at the first fret

Measuring the string height
at the tenth Fret

String Height from the Top of the Fret to the Bottom of the String

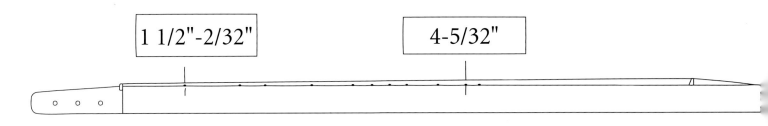

1 1/2"-2/32"   4-5/32"

Chapter 14
Inlay

Incorporating an inlay on your pickin' stick is a way to personalize the instrument and express your creativity. While an inlay is optional, you will find that doing this will elevate your skills. It is not as difficult as it might appear. Most inlay material on stringed instruments is mother-of-pearl shell or abalone shell. These are available from luthier supply companies in random size pieces about .050" thick.

The darker the wood on the instrument, the more invisible the lines from the routed cavity will be, so consider this in your design. It would be a good idea to practice on a scrap piece of wood before doing the final inlay on your instrument.

Inlay Tools

There are just a few specialty tools needed for basic inlay work. To cut out the shell, you will need a jeweler's saw (A) with a fine blade (40 to 50 teeth per inch). A sharp scriber (B) is used to trace around the shell design into the wood. To rout out the inlay you will need a Dremel® (C) tool with a precision router base (D). NOTE: The base that comes with the Dremel® kit is not accurate enough for inlay work. A board with a slot on one end (E) is used to hold the shell (F) while cutting. To do the best work possible you will want to use a magnifier (G) to see the cutting and routing up close. A small file (H) will help clean up the edges of the shell after cutting.

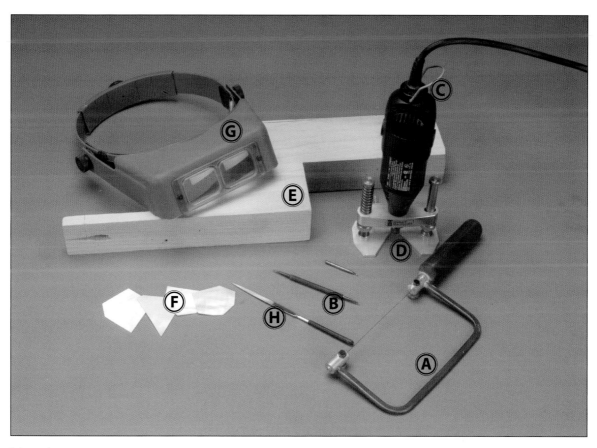

Inlay tools

The pattern you choose to inlay should be drawn on paper or printed on a computer. This pattern is glued to the shell and will be used as a guide while cutting the design out of the shell. Follow the steps shown here in the order shown and you will be surprised how easily you can do inlay work.

Laying out the desired inlay design on mother-of-pearl shell

Applying glue to inlay pattern

Gluing inlay pattern to shell

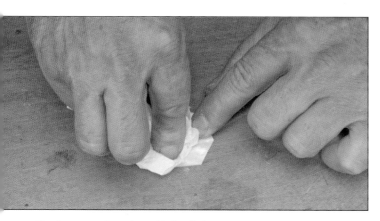

Pressing pattern into place with dry cloth

Drilling starter hole for inside cut

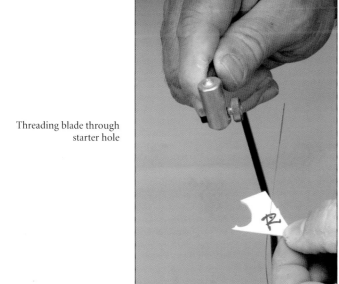

Threading blade through starter hole

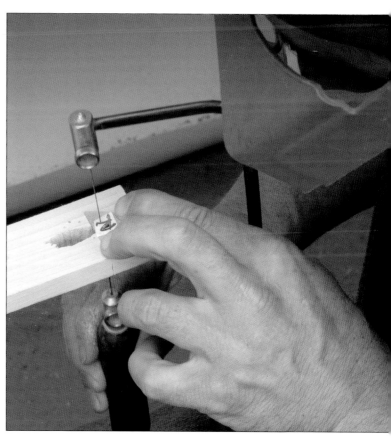

Cutting inside of inlay

Cutting outside of inlay

61

Letter cut out

Filing edges with small file

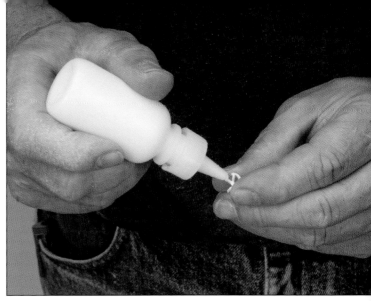

Gluing back side of inlay

Gluing inlay in position

Scribing around edges of inlay

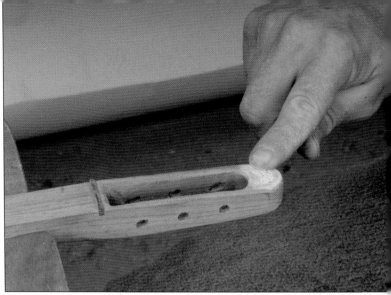

Working the chalk into the scribe lines

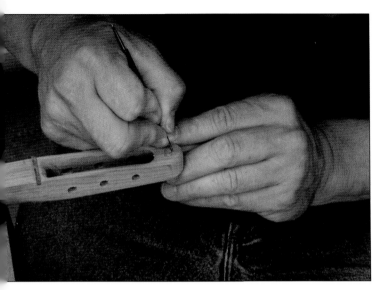

Scribing lines deeper after inlay is removed

Ready to rout out inlay cavity

Chalking the scribe lines

Setting depth of router bit

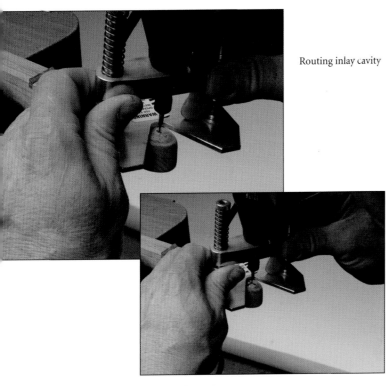

Routing inlay cavity

Routing inlay cavity

Making fine sawdust to fill the voids

Sawdust on inlay for filler

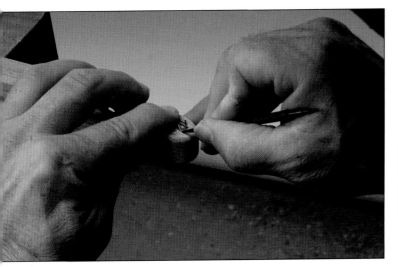

Checking fit of inlay

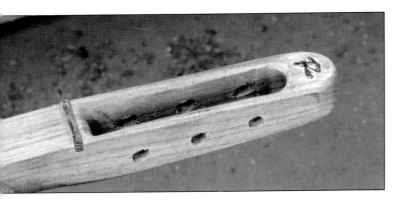

Inlay fit into the inlay cavity

Working the sawdust filler into the voids

Inlay ready for gluing

Applying thin super glue to inlay

Final sanding of inlay

Glue on the inlay

Sanding the inlay flush

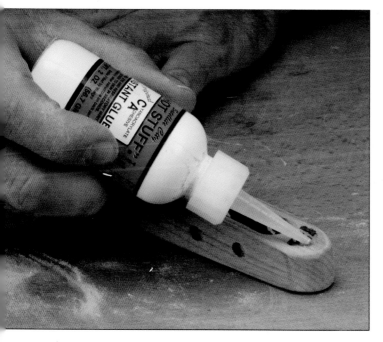

Applying second round of thin super glue

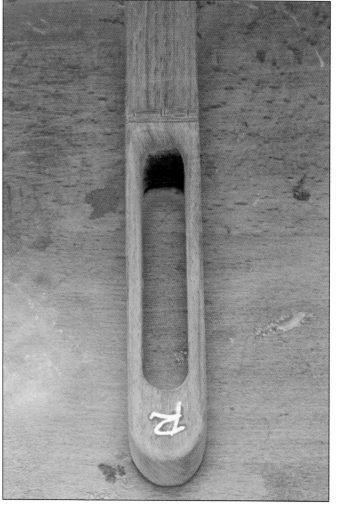

Completed inlay

Chapter 15
Finishing

Types of Finish

There are a variety of finishes that are appropriate for your pickin' stick. An oil finish will give a smooth satin finish that will allow your hand to move easily along the neck. Shellac, polyurethane, or lacquer will all provide a beautiful protective finish as well. As with any finishing process, make sure you are working in a well-ventilated area and are wearing a respirator.

Various types of appropriate finishes

sanding with 120-grit sandpaper. Follow this with 150-, 180-, and finally 220-grit. There is no need to sand higher than 220-grit. If you make the wood too smooth, the finish will not adhere to it as well.

Removing all hardware

Final Sanding to 220- or 320-grit sandpaper

Preparation

You have probably been enjoying playing your pickin' stick and will be reluctant to take the strings off for finishing. However, you will need to look ahead and think of how the finish will show off the beautiful wood that you carefully selected and display your fine craftsmanship.

Remove all hardware including the end pins, tuners, and strings. Place all of the small screws and brads in a small bag so they will not get lost. Now it is time to do a final sanding. If you can still see some saw marks or planer marks, start

Final Inspection

When you feel you are finished sanding, give the instrument a final inspection with your magnifier. Perform this inspection with good lighting. Look for any scratches or gaps between the joints. If you find a small gap, fill the gap with sawdust and put a drop of thin super glue on top. Have a paper towel ready to dab off the excess if needed. Now sand this area down. The gap will be invisible and will not show through finish.

Final inspection with magnifier and light

Gap that needs to be filled

Filling gap with sawdust and thin super glue

Completed gap fill

Masking the Frets

We don't want to allow finish to get on the frets, so we will need to mask them off. Use painters tape to cover the frets. For each fret, cut a piece of tape that is a little longer than the fret. Place the tape over the fret so that it is completely covered. Run your fingernail along the sides of the fret for a good fit. Use a razor blade to score the tape on both sides of the frets. Finally, cut the tape at the ends of the fret.

Masking the frets

Trimming fret mask with razor blade

Sealing

A seal coat provides a good base for the final finish and keeps the finish from soaking into the wood. This will be especially important for the softer spruce top. Shellac sealer is a good choice for a seal coat as it will adhere to most materials and most finishes will adhere very well to shellac.

After the seal coat has dried, scuff sand it with 220-grit sandpaper. Scuff sanding is a light sanding that will knock down the wood fibers that have been raised due to the moisture in the shellac. You will need to scuff sand between coats of the final finish as well.

Applying a Finish

When spraying, it works best to hang the instrument from the end so that you can spray all sides of the instrument at the same time. You can insert an eye screw in the end block to hang it. It is better to spray numerous light coats rather than a few heavy coats to prevent drips and runs. If you are using a polyurethane finish, two to three coats will be sufficient. Be sure to scuff sand in between each coat with 220- or 320-grit sandpaper.

Final Steps

Allow the finish to harden for a few days to a week You can now polish the instrument with some 0000 steel wool. This will give it a nice smooth feel that you can be proud of. Once you are satisfied with the finish, it is time to remove the fret masks. You may need to score both sides of the fret with a razor blade to remove it without chipping.

Now it is time to re-install the hardware and the strings. If you would like, you can place a small piece of felt under the strings where they go over the end of the instrument in order to help protect the top.

You are now a proud owner of your very own hand-crafted instrument. You will probably need to plan to make a few more since your family members and friends will claim it as their own.

Chapter 16
Tuning and Playing

The pickin' stick strings are tuned to G D G (near middle C on a keyboard) as shown here. You can use a piano or another instrument for tuning. The best device for stringed instruments, however, is a digital tuner. It is an easy way to keep your instrument tuned accurately. A digital tuner simply clips on the headstock of the instrument and picks up the vibrations directly from the instrument when the string is plucked. The digital display will show what note is being played. It will also show if the string is flat or sharp, which will help you determine if you need to tighten or loosen the string to get it in tune. This device simplifies the tuning process and will erase much frustration in tuning the instrument.

Open G Tuning

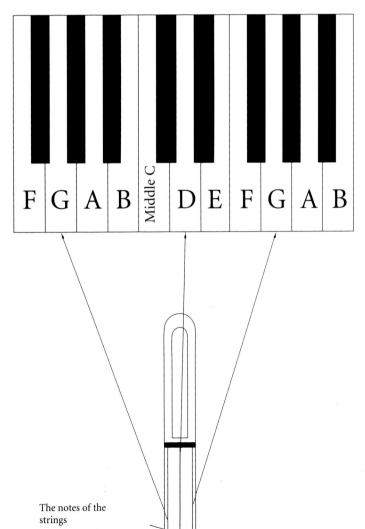

The notes of the strings

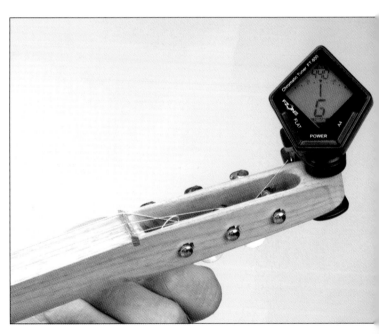

Tuning with a digital tuner

Getting Started Playing

The fingerboard of the pickin' stick has a diatonic scale, which allows you to play easy melodies without any complex fingering arrangements. Since the pickin' stick is tuned to an open G tuning, any note you play will sound good. Typically, the bottom string (.010) is the melody string.

To play your pickin' stick, simply press this string down to the fingerboard between any fret location and strum all of the strings with a pick. The other two strings will blend with the melody note to produce an automatic chord. Now move your finger to another fret location and strum all of the strings again. You will soon begin to see how to move your fingers from fret to fret to pick out a melody.

Dulcimer tablature can be used, but it will read backwards from the pickin' stick since the dulcimer's melody string is the top string. I would encourage you to learn to play by ear and pick out the notes to a song. Once you work with this for a while, you will soon begin to hear melodies and be able to pick them out without the help of a book

Once you become comfortable picking out a melody, you can learn different chord combinations that will allow you to strum along with other instruments. Several chord combinations are shown here. Once you learn one chord formation, you can play this same formation anywhere on the neck.

Playing the melody string

Playing a chord

Pickin' Stick Chord Chart

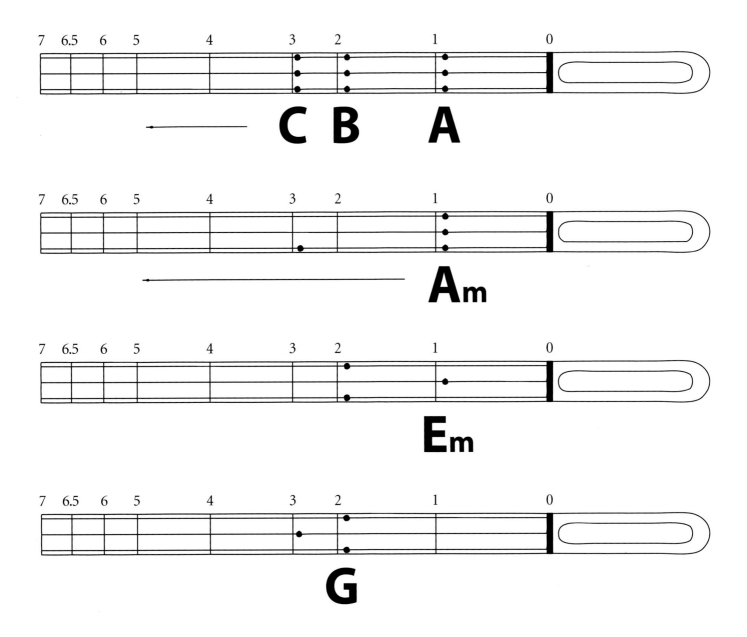

Pickin' Stick Chord Chart

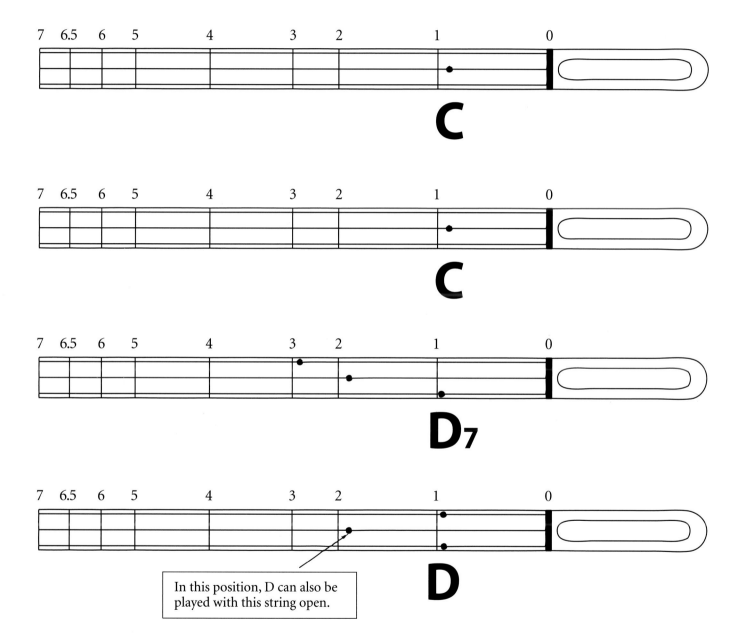

In this position, D can also be played with this string open.

RESOURCES

Stewart McDonald
www.stewmac.com
Luther's tools, materials, books, and kits

Luthier's Mercantile International, Inc
www.lmii.com
Luther's tools, materials, books, and kits

Musicmaker's Kits
www.harpkit.com
Instrument kits, plans, parts, instructional books

Elderly Instruments
Mandolin tuners, strings, instruments, and books
www.elderly.com

McNally Instruments
www.strumstick.com
Instruments and instructional books